to: _____

from:_____

D1443203

JUST ANOTHER DAY...

in the Office of the Damned

Published by Sellers Publishing, Inc.
161 John Roberts Road, South Portland, ME 04106
Visit us at www.sellerspublishing.com • E-mail: rsp@rsvp.com

 Like Us on Facebook

Copyright © Sellers Publishing, Inc.
Art & Text © 2014 Ephemera

ISBN-13: 978-1-4162-4528-5

Printed and bound in China.

10 9 8 7 6 5 4 3 2 1

JUST ANOTHER DAY...
in the Office of the Damned

SELLERS
PUBLISHING

Rest assured, Cindy, that all your effort and hard work *will* go unnoticed.

I always take work
with a grain of salt –
plus a slice of lime and
a shot of tequila.

Do I look like a freaking information desk?

I never make the same mistake twice. I make it five or six times, just to be sure.

Dear God, Will someone please die so I can get a promotion?

I hate my job enough to constantly bitch about it, but not enough to actually look for another one.

THINGS TO DO:
1. Procrastinate
2. Panic

Like they pay me
enough to care.

Pride.
Teamwork.
Effort.
We'll have none
of that bullshit
around here.

Just another day . . .
in the office of the damned.

Going to Hell when I
die would be redundant.

You could file a
complaint, but my
supervisor doesn't
care either.

The only thing I inspire my staff to do is call in sick.

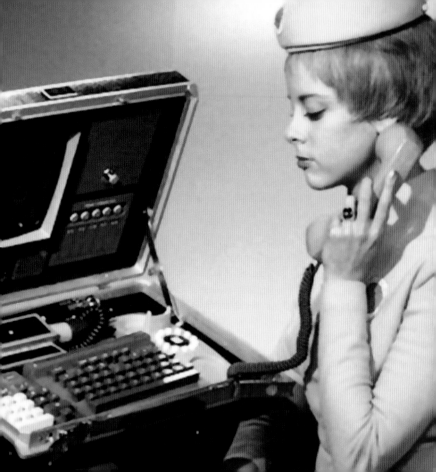

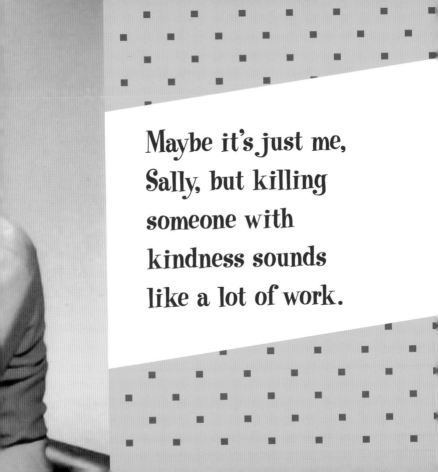

I'm out of bed and dressed.
What more do you want?

Just pretend
I'm not here.
That's what I do.

Why do I have to
go to work again?
I didn't do
anything wrong.

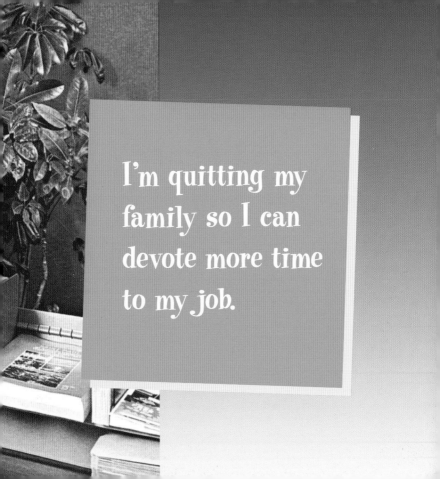

You can name your
own salary here.
I call mine Fred.

Don't worry.
We've dealt with
idiots before.

I'll forward this immediately . . to a department that gives a shit.

I haven't lost my mind –
it's in a file somewhere.

I used up all my sick days, so I'm calling in dead.

"Teamwork" means never having to take all the blame.

All this,
and minimum
wage too!

Based on my calculations, I can retire about five years after I die.

Why won't they
just fire me?

Well, if I'm not fired,
can I have the day off?

I want to thank all the
little people who kiss my ass.